HAWKS & FALCONS

BY MARIA MUDD RUTH

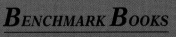

BENCHMARK BOOKS

MARSHALL CAVENDISH
NEW YORK

Series Consultant

James G. Doherty

General Curator, Bronx Zoo, New York

Thanks to Dr. Christine Sheppard, ornithology curator, Wildlife Conservation Society, Bronx, New York,

for her expert reading of this manuscript.

Benchmark Books

Marshall Cavendish

99 White Plains Road

Tarrytown, NY 10591–9001

www.marshallcavendish.com

Library of Congress Cataloging–in–Publication Data

Ruth, Maria Mudd

Hawks and falcons / by Maria Mudd Ruth.

p. cm. – (Animals, animals)

Summary: Describes the physical characteristics, behavior, habitat, and endangered status of hawks and falcons.

Includes bibliographical references and index.

ISBN 0-7614-1616-1

1. Hawks–Juvenile literature. 2. Falcons–Juvenile literature.

[1. Hawks. 2. Falcons. 3. Endangered species.] I. Title. II. Series.

QL696.F32M84 2003

598.9'44–dc21

2003001435

Photo Research by Anne Burns Images
Cover Photo by: Peter Arnold/Fred Bruemmer
The photographs in this book are used with the permission and through the courtesy of: *Animals,Animals*: Robert H. Armstrong 4, 27; Alan G. Nelson 10 (lower); Zig Leszczynski, 12; Reed/Williams, 17; Survi D.Green,.20; Tim Kimmel, 38. *Visuals Unlimited*: Gilbert Twiest, 6; Fritz Polking, 10 (upper). *Peter Arnold*: Robert H. Armstrong, 9; Galen Powell, 14; John Cancalosi, 22; Dr. Harvey Barnett, 28; Gerard Lacz, 32; Georges Dif, 41. *Corbis*: Jonathan Blair, 36; W. Perry Conway, 42.

Printed in China

1 3 5 6 4 2

On the cover: Gyrfalcon in white winter plumage on the Arctic tundra.

CONTENTS

1

INTRODUCING HAWKS AND FALCONS

High above you in the wide–open sky is the small, dark shape of a bird. It is soaring in wide circles above a meadow. You follow it closely with your eyes. Its wings are not moving. It seems to float on the air, circling. Then you hear it call–*keeeeer! keeeeer!* The bird begins to circle lower and lower. It flaps its broad wings several times. You can see the brown and white feathers of its wings and body. Then you see something you never imagined.

It stops flapping its wings and hovers motionless above the ground for a moment. Then it plunges down-ward toward the ground headfirst. You think it is going to crash. But just a few feet above the ground, the bird swoops upward, extending its sharp claws down toward the ground. Then it swoops back up–with a mouse in its grip. It flaps its wings and rises up into the sky. Soon it is

A NORTHERN HARRIER GLIDES GRACEFULLY TO A LANDING IN THE ALASKAN WILDERNESS. HAWKS AND FALCONS ARE ADMIRED WORLDWIDE AS POWERFUL FLIERS AND SKILLED HUNTERS.

FROM ITS PERCH IN A TALL SAGUARO CACTUS, A RED-TAILED HAWK SURVEYS ITS DESERT SURROUNDINGS IN THE SOUTHWESTERN UNITED STATES. HAWKS AND FALCONS LIVE ON MOST CONTINENTS OF THE WORLD, IN A WIDE RANGE OF HABITATS.

a small, dark shape. Then it is out of sight. You have just witnessed the beauty and power of a red–tailed hawk.

Like other hawks and their close relatives the falcons, this red–tailed hawk is a *bird of prey*. Birds of prey are birds that hunt live animals and insects, called prey, for food. Other birds of prey include eagles, buzzards, kites, and owls. These birds are also called *raptors*.

There are over two hundred different *species*, or kinds, of hawks and some sixty species of falcons in the world. Hawks and falcons can be found on every continent except Antarctica. They live in grasslands, forests, prairies, deserts, seacoasts, and the Arctic tundra. In these places, called *habitats*, hawks and falcons have all the living and nonliving things they need to live and grow. Because these natural habitats are disappearing as human popu-lations expand, some hawks and falcons live in cities where they make their homes in parks and on the tops of tall buildings.

Hawks and falcons are *diurnal* hunters, which means they are active during the day. This makes it easier for us to observe them. But even with binoculars, it can be difficult to identify hawks and falcons. Many species have similar body shapes and coloring. Many fly so swiftly that we can-not get a good look at them. And, because these birds are closely related, there are hawks that behave like falcons, and falcons that behave like hawks. Their names can be confusing, too. The peregrine falcon is often called a "duck hawk." The American kestrel is a falcon nicknamed "sparrow hawk." The osprey is a hawk sometimes called a "fish hawk."

One way to get to know hawks and falcons is to learn about their lives as hunters. An osprey, for example, hunts fish in lakes, rivers, and oceans all over the world. It is a large hawk with a wingspan of up to 6 feet. When it hunts, it cruises slowly above the water then plunges straight down, feetfirst into the water, after its prey. Because it is a large hawk, it can handle fish weighing an average of 2 pounds (1 kilogram). Grasping its meal in sharp, curved claws, called *talons*, the osprey flies up off the water and then shakes like a dog in midair to dry off.

Most hawks hunt alone, but the Harris's hawk, which lives in the deserts of North and South America, has a different style. Around sunrise and sunset, when the

AN OSPREY HAS A REVERSIBLE TOE ON EACH FOOT THAT CAN BE MOVED TO FACE BACKWARD FOR AN EXTRA-TIGHT GRIP ON SLIPPERY FISH.

A PEREGRINE FALCON CHICK AND ADULT MAKE THEIR HOME ON THE LEDGE OF A TALL BUILDING IN NEW YORK CITY. SCIENTISTS HAVE DISCOVERED THAT THESE CLIFF-DWELLING BIRDS CAN SURVIVE IN CITIES WHERE PIGEONS ARE ABUNDANT AND EASY PREY.

THE OSPREY'S WHITE UNDERSIDE DISAPPEARS AGAINST THE SKY AS IT FLIES ABOVE LAKES, RIVERS, AND BAYS IN ITS HUNT FOR FISH. ITS FIERCE FEET HAVE TWO TOES THAT EXTEND FORWARD AND TWO THAT EXTEND BACKWARD, SO IT CAN GRIP FIRMLY ONTO SLIPPERY FISH.

temperatures are cooler, Harris's hawks will gather together in groups of five or six. Together they will hunt animals such as jackrabbits, which can be too large for one bird to handle. The hunters share the work as well as the feast. One jackrabbit can feed five or six hawks.

The Aplomado falcon is a hunter of the open grass–lands and savannas of North and South America. It hunts small mammals, reptiles, birds, and insects. It grabs insects out of the air and eats them while flying. Chasing birds in the air or on the ground, the Aplomado follows them into the brush. During grass fires, this clever falcon will fly back and forth in front of the fire to catch escaping insects and other animals.

People have long admired the hunting skills of hawks and falcons. Three thousand years ago in Asia people cap–tured goshawks, peregrine falcons, and kestrels, training the birds to hunt for them. These birds would perch on thick leather wristbands on their owners' arms then fly off to hunt rabbits, partridges, and other small animals. A well–trained bird would catch prey and return with it to its owner's arm. The sport of falconry became popular in Europe and in North America where it is still practiced.

THE SMALLEST FALCON IN NORTH AMERICA, THE AMERICAN KESTREL HUNTS INSECTS AND SMALL MAMMALS SUCH AS MICE. THESE FALCONS OFTEN HUNT FROM PERCHES IN TREES OR ON TELEPHONE WIRES IN OPEN AREAS.

It is a thrill to watch a hawk or falcon soaring in the sky or diving toward the earth. You might also spot a hawk perched in a tree or on a telephone wire. Though they are not as abundant as sparrows or finches, hawks and falcons are all around us.

2

HAWK OR FALCON?

Hawks and falcons have much in common. Both are diurnal birds of prey with powerful eyesight. The power comes partly from the large size of their eyes, which in many species are larger and heavier than human eyes are. Hawks and falcons have eyes placed toward the front of their heads, rather than on the sides. This gives them what is called *binocular* vision–the ability to use both eyes at the same time to focus on one object. This helps them focus clearly and quickly at different distances. A red–tailed hawk, for example, can locate a mouse moving in the grass hundreds of feet away. It will then stay focused on the rodent until close enough to pounce on it. Unlike many other kinds of birds, hawks and falcons can see well both straight ahead and to the sides. Calling a person "hawk–eyed" means he or she can see things at great distances–often before anyone else can.

Hawks and falcons are skilled hunters. Among their

IDENTIFYING HAWKS AND FALCONS IN THE WILD CAN BE CHALLENGING. THE PEREGRINE FALCON HAS EVENLY STRIPED UNDERWINGS AND A DISTINCTIVE DARK "MUSTACHE" THAT HELPS BIRDERS RECOGNIZE IT.

many different hunting styles, some species capture prey by making a steep dive from a great height. This behavior is called *stooping* and is extremely exciting to witness. Peregrine falcons are one of the fastest birds on earth. Scientists have recorded them stooping at over 200 miles per hour (320 kilometers/hour).

Hawks and falcons have heavy, strong feet. They strike with their talons open and often kill their prey on impact. Talons are powerful hunting tools that can pierce or crush the body of the bird's prey. They can also hold the prey firmly while the bird is eating it. Hawks and falcons both have short, hooked beaks for gripping and tearing. Small birds, like the American kestrel, have short beaks for eating insects and other small animals. Large birds, like the gyr–falcon, have larger beaks for killing larger prey such as ducks and geese. If the prey is another bird, the hawk or falcon will pluck the feathers before eating it. If the prey is a reptile or animal covered in fur, the hawks and falcons strip off enough skin and fur to expose the flesh.

Telling the difference between a hawk and a falcon can

THE SHARP VISION OF HAWKS AND FALCONS ALLOWS THEM TO RECOGNIZE THEIR PREY AT TWO TO THREE TIMES THE DISTANCE THAT A HUMAN BEING CAN DETECT THE SAME CREATURE.

ALL HAWKS AND FALCONS HAVE SHARP EYESIGHT AND STRONG, HOOKED BEAKS. BRIGHT EYES WILL HELP THIS RED-TAILED HAWK SPOT PREY THAT IT WILL EASILY DEVOUR WITH ITS POWERFUL BEAK.

FALCONS

FALCONS HAVE LONG, POINTED WINGS AND LONG TAILS.

HARRIER

HARRIERS HAVE LONG, NARROW WINGS AND LONG TAILS.

OSPREY

OSPREYS ARE LARGE BIRDS WITH A CROOKED WING SHAPE. THE TOP OF THE WING IS ANGLED, MUCH LIKE THE WING OF A GULL.

SHARP-SHINNED HAWK

SHARP-SHINNED HAWKS, AND OTHER ACCIPITERS, HAVE SHORT WINGS AND LONG, SQUARE TAILS.

MOST OF THE HAWKS AND FALCONS WE SEE ARE IN FLIGHT FAR ABOVE OUR HEADS. SOMETIMES THEY ARE TOO FAR AWAY FOR US TO SEE THE PATTERNS OR COLORS OF THEIR FEATHERS. MANY BIRD WATCHERS CAN IDENTIFY A HAWK OR FALCON BY ITS SILHOUETTE OR BY THE OUTLINE OF ITS BODY, WINGS, AND TAIL.

be tricky. Even *ornithologists*, the scientists who study birds, cannot always tell them apart easily. Generally, falcons are slim birds with long tails and long, pointed wings built for speed. Their wing strokes are steady, strong, and rapid.

Most falcons hunt from tree perches or cliff edges in the open where their prey are likely to be. When a falcon spots its prey a high-speed chase begins. If its prey is a bird, the falcon will attack in midair and use its long hind toe, called "the killing toe," to strike its prey to the ground. If the prey is moving along the ground, the falcon will attack it there. Falcons kill their prey, which are often much larger than themselves, by biting the head or neck with a special tooth on its upper beak. The tooth fits into a notch in the bird's lower beak and is inserted along the prey's spine for the final bite.

Hawks have several different flying and hunting styles. Some hawks soar and circle high over open fields and forest edges to search for prey before diving toward it feetfirst. These hawks are called *buteos* and have long, broad wings and short, wide tails. The red-tailed hawk is a buteo. Other hawks have short, rounded wings and long tails. These are called *accipiters*, the hawks of the forest. Accipiters hunt from perches or by chasing their prey, taking the prey by surprise. Their short wings allow them

THE NORTHERN HARRIER NESTS ON THE GROUND AND IS WELL HIDDEN AMONG TALL PLANTS GROWING AROUND FIELDS, MEADOWS, AND MARSHES. WHEN HUNTING, HARRIERS FLY LOW OVER THE GROUND TO SEARCH FOR PREY BY SIGHT AND SOUND.

to twist and turn through the forest. Because they live and hunt in the forest, most accipiters are harder to observe than buteos. The sharp–shinned hawk, however, is an accipiter that visits backyard bird feeders where it preys on the birds feeding there.

The northern harrier, also called the "marsh hawk," might be the easiest hawk to identify because it flies so close to the ground. As it searches carefully for prey in fields and marshes, it seems to touch the ground with its body and hug the bushes with its wings. Scientists think that harriers hunt by sound as well as by sight. Like all birds, the harrier has large ear openings hidden behind the feathers on its face. The facial feathers of the harrier, however, are arranged in a disk shape like those of an owl. Ornithologists think that these disks of feathers help harriers locate prey by concentrating sounds. With a sudden pounce, harriers capture birds, frogs, reptiles, or small rodents such as the meadow vole.

3
LIFE CYCLE

Watching a single hawk or falcon soar, circle, hover, and stoop is one of the great thrills in nature. But these birds are not always alone. During the spring and summer, male and female birds begin their courtship behavior. They display their amazing flying skills to each other and per-form acrobatic loops and dives. Watch the skies closely during mating season and you may see quite a show.

Male and female red-tailed hawks will whirl through the sky, grappling with each other's talons, tumbling together in cartwheels or swinging together from side to side. A harrier performs "sky dances" by swooping up and down as if it were traveling along steep hills and valleys. It will climb each "hill" by flapping its wings, roll upside down at the top, turn right side up, then dive down the "valleys" on closed wings. A male osprey may rise up to 1,000 feet (300 m) in the air with a fish gripped in its talons. It will display its fish, then dive down and fly back up to repeat the performance. What show-offs!

AN ADULT HARRIS'S HAWK FEEDS HER CHICK MORSELS OF FOOD IN THE SAFETY OF THEIR SAGUARO CACTUS NEST. IN THE ANIMAL KINGDOM, HAWKS AND FALCONS ARE KNOWN TO BE CARING PARENTS.

COURTSHIP DISPLAYS

DURING MATING SEASON, HAWKS AND FALCONS SHOW OFF THEIR FLYING SKILLS TO ATTRACT MATES AND MARK THEIR TERRITORIES. DIFFERENT SPECIES OF BIRDS FLY DIFFERENT PATTERNS IN THE AIR. HERE IS ONE OF THE MOST ACROBATIC ONES:

MALE

FEMALE

A THE "SKY DANCES" OFTEN BEGIN WITH THE PARTNERS SOARING TOGETHER THROUGH THE SKY.

B THEN THE MALE MIGHT DIVE DOWN IN A MOCK ATTACK.

C THE FEMALE SOMETIMES FLIES UPSIDE DOWN FOR A SHORT TIME, TOUCHING THE TALONS OF HER MATE.

D THE PAIR THEN RETURNS TO SOARING AND MAY REPEAT THE SEQUENCE.

During mating season, hawks and falcons will become quite loud to help them attract mates. Goshawks will call *kak-kak-kak-kak*, peregrine falcons a harsh *cack-cack-cack*, kestrels a *kleee-kleee*. Harriers will whistle. Red–tails will yelp. They also make these calls to mark and defend their territories and nests.

After a female and male pair up, they mate and occupy their nesting site. Falcons do not build their own nests. They move into the abandoned stick nests of crows, hawks, and other birds. Some falcons scrape or scratch the bare ground with their feet to make a shallow bowl in the dirt called a *scrape*. These scrapes are often hidden under bushes, but gyrfalcons and peregrine falcons make their scrapes on cliff ledges. American kestrels, the smallest North American falcons, prefer a bit more protection. They nest in abandoned woodpecker holes, under barn roofs, and in cavities in cliffs. Kestrels are the only falcons that will use man–made nest boxes.

Hawks are nest builders. They build large stick nests on

HAWKS AND FALCONS OFTEN USE THE SAME NESTING SITE FOR MANY GENERATIONS. IN BRITAIN, CERTAIN CLIFFS HAVE BEEN USED BY PEREGRINE FALCONS FOR 300 YEARS.

AN OSPREY PERCHES ON ITS LARGE STICK NEST BUILT ATOP A TALL, DEAD TREE. THE FEMALE OSPREY WILL LAY AND INCUBATE TWO TO FOUR EGGS WHILE THE MALE HUNTS, RETURNING TO THE NEST TO EAT WHAT HE HAS CAUGHT.

ONLY FIVE WEEKS OLD, THESE RED-SHOULDERED HAWKS KEEP WARM WITH THICK, DOWNY FUR. TOO YOUNG TO FLY AND HUNT, THEY MUST WAIT FOR THEIR PARENTS TO FEED THEM.

rock ledges or sturdy tree branches. Many nests are used year after year for many generations. Ospreys nest in the tops of trees and on tall wooden man–made platforms placed on docks or riverbanks. Some osprey nests weigh several hundred pounds. Desert–dwelling Harris's hawks build their nests in the crotch of tall saguaro cactuses. Harriers nest on the ground, usually on a platform of sticks, grass, or cattails. Some hawks are not very picky about where they nest as long as there is food nearby. A group of bird watchers discovered a red–tailed hawk nest on the window ledge of an apartment building in the middle of New York City. The birds hunted mostly pigeons, which are very common in the city and its parks.

Hawks and falcons lay from one to six eggs, depending on the species. The eggs are oval like chicken eggs with more pointed ends. This shape works well for birds that nest on ledges and cliffs because, when disturbed, the egg rolls in circles rather than away from the nest.

The female sits on the eggs to *incubate* them, or keep them warm until they hatch. In about thirty days the chicks hatch with thin coats of downy feathers. Both parents care for the chicks. In most cases, the male hunts for the family, bringing the food to the female in the nest. A male sharp–shinned hawk, however, brings the prey to a branch near the nest and calls to the female. When she arrives, he passes her the prey and she returns to the nest.

For the female harrier, getting the prey from her mate can be tricky. She must fly toward the male, turn upside down, and catch the prey in her talons as he drops it from above. Females of all species clean and shred the food into small pieces and feed it to their chicks. The female also protects the chicks from sun and rain and from predators such as owls, crows, raccoons, and snakes.

The young stay in the nest for up to two months. Their down becomes thick and fluffy, then is replaced gradually by feathers that make them look, and eventually fly, like their parents. They spend much of their time eating, learning how to shred their own meat, and getting ready for flight. After several weeks of flapping their wings in the nest and watching their parents fly, the young birds make their first flights. Even though they can fly, young hawks and falcons still depend on their parents for food for several more weeks. During this time, the young birds practice their flying and get hunting lessons from their parents. Many adults will fly near their chicks with prey in their talons and encourage the young to snatch it from them. Osprey parents teach their young to hunt by flying over the water, dropping fish in midair. Over and over, the young birds practice diving into the water to fetch the fish.

By the fall, most young hawks and falcons are able to hunt for food on their own. In their second year, they are ready to perform their own sky dances, continuing the cycle of life.

4
THE GREAT MIGRATION

After their first summer of learning the ways of the wind and sky, many young hawks and falcons make their first big journeys. The journey, called *migration*, is the regular movement of a large number of animals from one place to another, most often for a better food supply. Depending on the species of bird and where it lives, the migrations vary from hundreds to tens of thousands of miles. Most migrations start in fall or early winter when the weather turns colder and the supply of food begins to dwindle. Hawks and falcons migrate to warmer climates where the food is more plentiful. In the spring, when the warm weather and the prey animals return, the birds follow the same route home to mate and nest.

Depending on where you live, you might be able to watch hundreds or even thousands of migrating birds flying

WITH A WINGSPAN UP TO 47 INCHES (119 CM), THE MAJESTIC GYRFALCON IS THE LARGEST FALCON IN NORTH AMERICA. IT MAKES ITS HOME ON THE ARCTIC TUNDRA, WHERE THE SNOWY LANDSCAPE CAMOUFLAGES ITS WHITE PLUMAGE.

overhead on a beautiful autumn day. Some species migrate in flocks, others alone. Unlike most songbirds that migrate at night, hawks and falcons migrate during the day. Because many hawks and falcons soar on natural currents of warm air that rise in the daytime, most do not fly at night or in the rain when the warmer air falls. Before sunset, they hunt. After sunset, they settle on trees and other perches and rest for the night. Hawks and falcons avoid migrating over large bodies of water by flying along sea–coasts, lakeshores, and the edges of mountain ranges.

During summer in the Arctic, gyrfalcons prey upon lemmings, rabbits, other small mammals, and large birds. In the fall, when its prey hibernates or migrates, the gyrfalcon leaves its dark and frozen homeland. It flies south into Canada and the northern United States for food. Gyrfalcons have been spotted as far south as Virginia, Kansas, Texas, and California.

Sharp–shinned hawks migrate from the northern part of the United States and Canada, southward across the continent as far as southern Florida and Central America. Groups of peregrine falcons move southward along the Atlantic coast and can be seen in places such as Cape May, New Jersey and Assateague Island along the Maryland and Virginia shores.

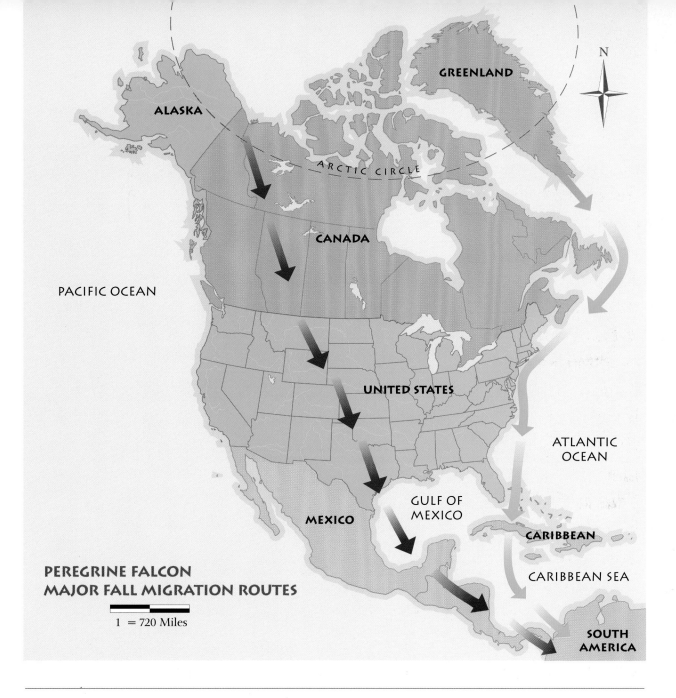

PEREGRINE FALCON
MAJOR FALL MIGRATION ROUTES

1 = 720 Miles

KNOWN TO BE THE FASTEST BIRD ON THE EARTH, THE PEREGRINE FALCON ALSO FLIES GREAT DISTANCES DURING ITS SPRING AND FALL MIGRATIONS. SCIENTISTS STUDYING PEREGRINES OF THE ARCTIC TUNDRA HAVE TRACKED SOME BIRDS THOUSANDS OF MILES AWAY IN ARGENTINA.

BIRD WATCHERS FLOCK TOGETHER IN THE MOUNTAINS OF PENNSYLVANIA EACH AUTUMN TO WATCH HUNDREDS OF HAWKS SOAR PAST. EACH YEAR, THE BIRDS FLY SOUTHWARD ALONG THE SAME MIGRATION PATHWAY.

36

Because hawks and falcons migrate regularly and during the day, this is one of the best times to watch for these birds. Every year, hundreds of bird watchers gather at certain special spots where they know great numbers of birds will fly overhead. There may be a birding club in your area that can tell you the best viewing spots and times.

5
MASTERS OF THE SKY

Hawks and falcons are at the top of many people's lists of favorite birds. They are also at the top of the many food chains, the invisible chains that link animals to what they eat and what eats them. As a group, hawks and falcons are predators of many different kinds of animals such as rabbits, mice, rats, toads, frogs, birds, reptiles, fish, and insects. Keeping populations of many of these animals under control is important. As predators, hawks and falcons play a very important role in the food chain and in the balance of nature.

Being at the top of the food chain does not mean hawks and falcons have no predators. Other birds of prey, such as the great horned owl, will hunt hawks and falcons. Crows, snakes, and raccoons will raid an unguarded nest and take eggs or chicks for food.

A RED-TAILED HAWK PERCHES ON THE PROTECTED ARM OF A LICENSED FALCONER WHO HAS TRAINED THIS BIRD TO HUNT FOR HIM. THERE ARE ABOUT 7,000 LICENSED FALCONERS IN THE UNITED STATES, WHERE A YOUNG PERSON CAN BEGIN TRAINING IN THE ANCIENT SPORT OF FALCONRY AT THE AGE OF FOURTEEN.

Even though people do not hunt and kill hawks and falcons for meat, we have been responsible for killing many of these birds. Because some hawks prey on farmyard chickens, they are hunted and shot as pests. Sometimes hunters mistake them for game birds, such as pheasants, and shoot them. Hawks and falcons are captured to satisfy people interested in falconry, and are killed and stuffed for people to display as symbols of power. Though it is illegal to capture or kill a falcon or hawk or destroy their eggs without the proper permits, this still happens all over the world. Many activities that are not illegal, such as building roads, homes, and stores, cause problems, too. To make room for these things, habitats are destroyed. Hawks and falcons lose much of the land and waterways they need to survive.

No falcon or hawk has the speed or strength to escape chemicals such as *DDT*. In the 1940s, farmers used DDT on their crops to control insect pests. The DDT washed off the plants and worked its way into the soil, into the water, and into other insects and animals. When hawks and falcons hunted and ate these animals, the DDT got into their bodies, too. In the 1970s, scientists discovered that the DDT in the birds was causing the shells of their eggs to become thin and break during incubation. Fewer and fewer hawks and

SYMBOL OF POWER AND SPEED, THIS PEREGRINE FALCON AWAITS RELEASE INTO THE WILD. NEARING EXTINCTION IN THE 1970S, MANY PEREGRINES ARE BEING HATCHED AND RAISED IN CAPTIVITY TO INCREASE THEIR CHANCES OF SURVIVAL.

THE FOREST HOLDS THE FUTURE FOR THIS YOUNG NORTHERN GOSHAWK.
THIS SPECIES AND MANY OTHER HAWKS AND FALCONS HUNT FOR PREY IN
AND AT THE EDGES OF THESE DISAPPEARING HABITATS.

falcons were being born and the population of many species fell quickly.

In the 1970s, peregrine falcons nearly vanished from the United States. After DDT was banned in 1972, scientists began raising young peregrines in captivity and releasing them into the wild. Their work has been a success. The peregrines are making a strong comeback and are no longer an endangered species. But this does not mean peregrines or any other falcon or hawk is safe from other poisons, other hunters, and other human behavior that threatens their survival. These majestic birds need our help and protection to make sure they have what they need to survive. We can help them by learning about them and respecting the forests, fields, rivers, lakes, and marshes where they make their homes. Everyone should have the chance to look up in wonder at these masters of the sky.

accipiters: A group of hawks with short wings and long tails that hunt mostly in the forest by chasing their prey or attacking it by surprise.

binocular: Vision that uses both eyes at the same time to focus on an object.

bird of prey: A bird that hunts live animals and insects.

buteos: A group of hawks with broad wings and short tails that soar and circle to search for prey.

DDT: A chemical used to control insect pests.

diurnal: To be active during the day.

habitats: Places that have all the living and nonliving things that animals and other organisms need to live and grow.

incubate: To keep eggs warm before they hatch.

migration: The regular, seasonal movement of animals from one place to another, most often for a better food supply.

ornithologists: Scientists who study birds.

predators: Animals that hunt and kill other animals for food.

raptors: Another term for birds of prey.

scrape: A shallow hole scraped or scratched in the ground to be used as a nest.

species: A group of animals that can produce fertile offspring.

stooping: A flight behavior in which birds make very steep dives from great heights.

talons: The sharp, curved claws of many birds of prey.

BOOKS

Arnold, Carol. *Hawk Highway in the Sky: Watching Raptor Migration*. New York: Gulliver Books, 1997.

George, Jean Craighead. *My Side of the Mountain*. New York: Puffin Books, 2001.

Latimer, Jonathan P. and Karen Stray Nolting. *Birds of Prey (Peterson Field Guide for Young Naturalists)*. Boston: Houghton–Mifflin, 1999.

Miller, Millie. *Talons: North American Birds of Prey*. Boulder, CO: Johnson Books, 1989.

Olson, Penny. *Falcons and Hawks*. New York: Checkmark Books, 1992.

Price, Ann. *Raptors: The Eagles, Hawks, Falcons, and Owls of North America*. Lanham, MD: Roberts Rinehart, 2002.

Woodward, John. *Hawks and Falcons*. Tarrytown, NY: Benchmark Books, 1997.

WEBSITES

Hawkwatch International

www.hawkwatch.org

The Peregrine Fund

www.peregrinefund.org

The Pennsylvania Department of Environmental Protection

www.dep.state.pa.us/dep/falcon

Journey North

www.lerner.org/jnorth/

ABOUT THE AUTHOR

Maria Mudd Ruth is the author of several natural history books for young adults, including *Snakes, The Deserts of the Southwest, The Mississippi River, The Pacific Coast* (all Benchmark Book titles), and the *Ultimate Ocean Book*. She is currently writing a book on a mysterious seabird of the Pacific Coast.

I
N
D
E
X

Page numbers for illustrations are in **boldface.**